J.R.R. TOLKIEN

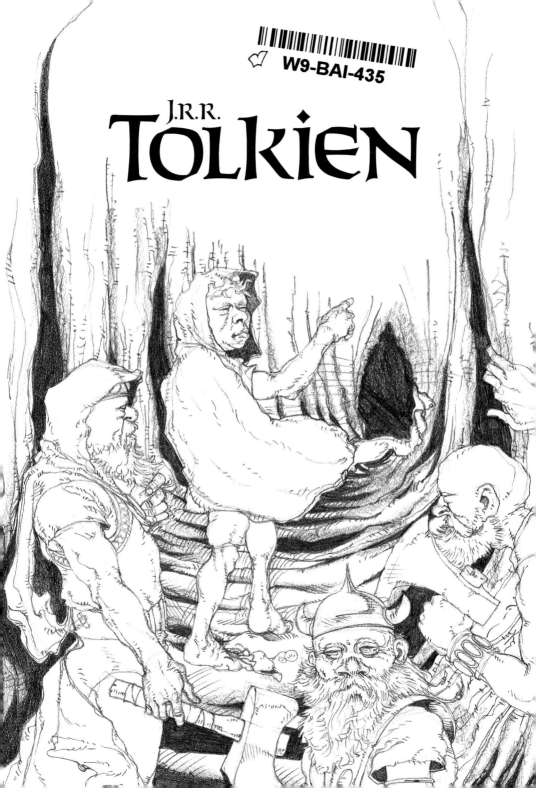

J.R.R. TOLKIEN

MASTER OF FANTASY

by DAVID R. COLLINS

ILLUSTRATED BY WILLIAM HEAGY

LERNER PUBLICATIONS COMPANY ◆ MINNEAPOLIS

Acknowledgments

The photographs in this book are reproduced through the courtesy of: Bettmann, pp. 60 (top), 75, 93 (both), 94, 95; British Tourist Authority, pp. 38, 54 (bottom), 92; David Dettman, pp. 76, 78, 84 (left), 88, 96 (both), 102; Exeter College, Oxford, pp. 42, 48, 49; Douglas R. Gilbert, pp. 69, 91, 97, 98; Imperial War Museum, p. 60; King Edward's School, Birmingham, pp. 21, 22, 29, 30 (both), 33; Library of Congress, p. 89; "Lord of the Rings: Fellowship of the Ring" Copyright 2000, New Line Productions, Inc.™ The Saul Zaentz Company d/b/a Tolkien Enterprises under license to New Line Productions, Inc. All rights reserved. Photo appears courtesy of New Line Productions, Inc., p. 103; Mansell Collection, pp. 37, 54 (top), 55 (both), 57, 58; National Archives, p. 61; SATOUR, p. 13; University of Leeds, p. 73; Linda Watt, p. 84 (right).

This book is available in two editions:
Library binding by Lerner Publications Company,
    a division of Lerner Publishing Group
Soft cover by First Avenue Editions,
    an imprint of Lerner Publishing Group
241 First Avenue North
Minneapolis, MN 55401 U.S.A.

Website address: www.lernerbooks.com

Library of Congress Cataloging-in-Publication Data

Collins, David R.
    J. R. R. Tolkien: Master of Fantasy / by David R. Collins
        p.   cm.
    Includes bibliographical references and index
    Summary: Describes the life of J. R. R. Tolkien, creator of Middle-earth and author of "The Hobbit" and "Lord of the Rings."
    ISBN 0-8225-4906-9 (lib. bdg. : alk. paper)
    ISBN 0-8225-9618-0 (pbk. : alk. paper)
    1. Tolkien, J. R. R. (John Ronald Reuel), 1892–1973—Juvenile literature. 2. Fantastic fiction, English—History and criticism—Juvenile literature. 3. Authors, English—20th century—Biography—Juvenile literature [1. tolkien, J. R. R. (John Ronald Reuel), 1892–1973. 2. Authors, English.] I. Title.
PR6039.032Z6228 1991
828'.91209—dc20   90-46766

Manufactured in the United States of America
3 4 5 6 7 8 – JR – 07 06 05 04 03 02

Contents

preface

Shortly after beginning my career as an English teacher in the early 1960s, I was introduced to J. R. R. Tolkien. No, it was not a face-to-face encounter but rather a meeting through the book reports my students were writing. My university studies had been rich and heavy with offerings in British literature, and I felt I could call Chaucer, Shakespeare, and Dickens by their first names. Yet Tolkien was a stranger to me, a complete unknown. But as the decade wore on and the number of Tolkien book reports increased, I knew I had to learn more about this man and his work. Young Americans were listening to one British import, the Beatles, but a substantial number of those same young Americans were reading J. R. R. Tolkien. Surely I should too.

Little did I anticipate the depth and breadth of the mission. To begin with, there is no need to continue weight-lifting in the local gym. Simply ask a friendly librarian to bring you a few of Tolkien's books. His is "heavy stuff" indeed, in every sense. Once you have carted the volumes to a nearby table, a light sweat covers your body. However, as you open the pages of a Tolkien offering, you will find your efforts rewarded. Prepare to visit another world, filled with fantastic characters, elaborate settings, exciting events. What magic Tolkien works with words and phrases; what images he creates! Surely if you were to look up the word *imagination* in the dictionary, a picture of Tolkien should accompany the definition.

As one reads the works of Tolkien, it is impossible not to wonder about the person who created such volumes. Although Tolkien himself believed that "the investigation of an author's life reveals very little of the workings of his mind," this does not stifle the curiosity. Over the years, countless students have posed questions about J. R. R. Tolkien. As a full-time English teacher who enjoys writing biographies, Tolkien seemed a natural subject.

In the pages that follow are the results of that labor. I hope that it honestly and usefully captures a brief word portrait of an extraordinary man.

Naturally I have drawn from many research sources. Humphrey Carpenter's authorized biography, *Tolkien,* has provided immeasurable information and insight. King Edward's School generously provided information on Tolkien's school career as well as copies of *King Edward's School Chronicle.* Other published volumes and printed references are included in the bibliography.

I would be remiss if I did not mention the valuable input of three individuals. Through correspondence and interview, Ronald Eames, Professor Eliot Parker, and the late Dr. Frederick J. Swanson provided treasured information and anecdotes based on their own association with and study of J. R. R. Tolkien.

To my editor, Mary Winget, a special thanks.

Enough of this. A fresh set of book reports waits for me upon my desk. Hopefully, Bilbo Baggins has met another young friend.

David R. Collins

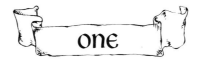

BEGINNINGS

High above the grasslands of South Africa, a full moon played hide-and-seek with the clouds. Somewhere in the shadows below, a pack of wolves howled eerily. A lone lion prowled silently, sniffing the air and searching for prey. Snakes silently slithered in the moonlight.

Meanwhile, the people in the town of Bloemfontein slept, some more restfully than others. Most of the inhabitants were of German, Dutch, or English background. A European community in this mostly black territory, Bloemfontein, which had been settled for less than 50 years, was a mixture of old and new. The town boasted an assortment of stone-and-wood homes, churches, government buildings, a library, a hospital, and a variety of small shops around the town square. But the wind swirled dust from the crude dirt streets, and the city park left much to be desired, according to one town resident, Mabel Tolkien.

Mabel and her husband, Arthur, were a handsome couple, known among their Bloemfontein neighbors for their tasteful dress and good manners. Mabel's soft reddish hair, piled neatly on top of her head—a popular style at that time—won frequent compliments, and she enjoyed the attention. The Tolkiens spent much time together. Some people remarked that they always seemed like newlyweds.

The arrival of a baby son on January 3, 1892, added extra joy. The child was named John after a grandfather, Ronald, simply because both parents liked it, and Reuel, which was his father's middle name. Ronald was the name that stuck firmly (at least in family circles), but all his life, he would enjoy doodling all four initials: J.R.R.T.

Arthur and Mabel Tolkien seldom let their baby out of their sight. They knew the dangers of the territory. Ronald experienced some frightening moments more than once during his early years. For example, one afternoon while the infant lay napping in the nursery, a neighbor's monkeys got into the nursery and chewed up three of the baby's pinafores.

Months later as Ronald struggled to take his first steps, he stumbled in the garden and fell near a tarantula. The spider bit the child and sent him crying and running across the open courtyard to his nurse. She did not waste a moment. She snatched Ronald up and immediately sucked out the poisonous venom. Luckily he suffered no ill effects.

But such frightening experiences did affect Mabel Tolkien. Monkeys, spiders, scorching heat waves, plagues of locusts—all led her to dislike Bloemfontein.

What had brought Mabel Suffield to South Africa in the first place? The question can be answered in one word—love. Mabel was only 17 when she met Arthur Tolkien in Birmingham, England. He was 30 and was seeking advancement in the world of banking. He had seen his father go bankrupt, and Arthur wanted no such future. After a quick courtship, the eager banker proposed marriage shortly after Mabel's 18th birthday. She accepted, but her father would not hear of a formal betrothal at her age. Arthur and Mabel were forced to wait before marrying. They shared their feelings through letters, which were carried and exchanged by Mabel's sister Jane.

Lloyds Bank in Birmingham offered Arthur Tolkien low wages and little hope for quick promotion. The discovery of diamonds and gold in South Africa promised brighter prospects for a better job in the banking business. Arthur found a position there.

At first Arthur traveled a great deal, but by the end of 1890, he was managing a branch of the Bank of Africa in Bloemfontein. The position paid well and provided a house in town. Arthur wrote to ask Mabel to come as soon as possible.

She prepared to leave soon after her 21st birthday. In March 1891, she packed her trunks, boarded the *Roslin Castle*, and sailed toward South Africa. Three weeks later, Mabel Suffield landed in Cape Town, and Arthur was there to greet her. A handsome figure he was, wearing a white suit and sporting a stylish moustache. Mabel and Arthur were married April 16, 1891.

After a brief honeymoon, the couple headed for Bloemfontein. The 700-mile (1,120-kilometer) journey was a trip into the past. Although some of the town's people lived fast-paced lives and competed for social position, there was also a relaxed mood about Bloemfontein. The Tolkien home, next door to the bank where Arthur worked, was spacious and comfortable, and Mabel even had servants to help her.

As the wife of a bank manager, Mabel entertained often. At first she enjoyed the social life, but she soon tired of the routine. Learning that she was pregnant lifted her spirits. The birth of Ronald in January 1892 delighted the couple, but soon afterward, Arthur began traveling again on business. A visit from Mabel's sister May brought memories of Birmingham racing back. Mabel longed to return to her family and friends in England.

On February 17, 1894, Mabel gave birth to a second child, Hilary Arthur Reuel Tolkien, and any thoughts of heading back to England were postponed. Hilary proved a stronger child than Ronald. Hilary adjusted quickly to both the climate and the dangers of Bloemfontein. But Ronald suffered during his teething period and from the extremes of hot and cold weather. The heat troubled him the most, and Mabel tried to find better conditions, at least for vacations. When Ronald was only three, his mother packed up both boys for a trip to Cape Town. There they enjoyed the sandy beaches and warm air.

One morning, shortly after returning to Bloemfontein, young Ronald found his father with a paintbrush in his hand. Arthur Tolkien painted letters A.R. TOLKIEN on the lid of a big trunk. He told Ronald that the trunk would soon be filled with clothes, ready for a voyage. The three-year-old boy smiled. He would never forget that particular moment with his father.

In April of 1895, Mabel Tolkien, with her two sons and their nurse, set sail for England. Within a month, they arrived in Birmingham. Although Birmingham is an industrial city of smokestacks and sprawling factories, Mabel was delighted to be home.

During the next few months, Ronald and Hilary received the hugs and kisses of relatives they had never seen before.

Cape Town is a major seaport in South Africa. The city lies at the foot of Table Mountain, which is seen in the background.

Grandfather Suffield, who had a long beard, was always ready with a quick joke. The old man loved playing with words—foolish nonsense, but what fun for young boys.

Arthur Tolkien remained in Bloemfontein, his letters always promising a future visit to England. Yet the months slipped by. At Christmas, Ronald and Hilary enjoyed a large, decorated Christmas tree for the first time. Until then the boys had viewed only a wilted eucalyptus tree at the Christmas holidays. Now they joined in singing cheerful carols and eating special holiday food.

In the midst of the festivities in Birmingham, Mabel received news that Arthur was ill. His illness overshadowed the holiday spirit, and Mabel quickly arranged to take her sons back to Bloemfontein. Despite the fun he had been having, Ronald welcomed the news that his mother was taking them

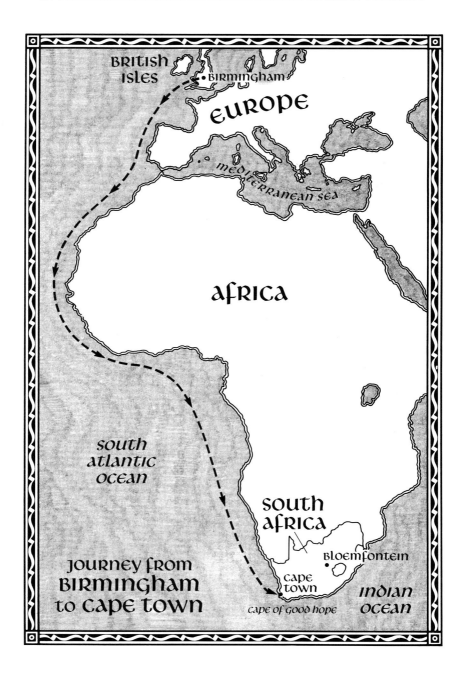

home. Ronald asked his nurse to write a letter from him to his father. In the letter, Ronald bragged that he was "a big man now," and promised to show his father all the Christmas presents he had received.

Before the letter could be sent, Arthur Tolkien suffered a severe hemorrhage and died on February 15, 1896. By the time his family learned of his death, he was already buried in a Bloemfontein graveyard 5,000 miles (8,000 km) away from Birmingham. Mabel was in a state of grief and confusion.

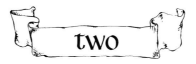

a world of words

Mabel Tolkien knew she couldn't remain permanently with her parents—not that Ronald and Hilary found such a life unpleasant. Ronald had grown especially fond of his grandfather. Often Ronald sat fascinated as the old man carefully drew a circle around a sixpenny coin and then proceeded to write every word of the Lord's Prayer inside the circle. Ronald could only print a few letters inside the small space. The old man also loved to tell tales of family history.

However, there was more to life than cheerful surroundings, word games, and amusing stories. Arthur Tolkien had left only a modest estate, and his widow needed more income to raise two young sons.

Someday Mabel Tolkien wanted both sons to enter King Edward's School, Birmingham's finest grammar school and the one their father had attended. But for the time being, the Tolkiens moved into a small brick cottage in the hamlet of Sarehole, a mile outside Birmingham. Ronald welcomed the fresh air and a chance to explore the countryside.

Ronald was able to read when he was only four, and he soon learned how to write as well. Thanks to Mabel's skills, he also began to learn Latin and French in addition to English. Mabel tried to teach Ronald to play the piano, but he showed no interest. Instead, words—regardless of their meanings—fascinated him. He delighted in their sounds and shapes.

Ronald liked drawing too. Most boys of his age could sit only a few minutes while working at a task, but Ronald could draw happily for hours with a sketch pad and pencil. Trees were a favorite subject. Perhaps he remembered the cedars and cypresses his father had planted in South Africa. Now in the English countryside, once Ronald finished drawing a tree, he climbed the tree, talked to it, and almost made it a special friend. When a weeping willow tree next to the nearby millpond was cut down, Ronald brooded for days.

Ronald enjoyed reading stories or having them read to him by his mother. *Alice in Wonderland* by Lewis Carroll and Andrew Lang's *Red Fairy Book* were among his favorites. When reading to him, his mother dared not skip a word or phrase—Ronald would catch her for certain. By the time he was seven, Ronald was writing stories of his own. His first story, which he remembered even after he had grown up, was about a "great green dragon."

In the fall of 1899, Ronald took the entrance exams for King Edward's School. Despite his abilities, he did not qualify and had to wait another year before trying again. The following year he passed. Since the school was four miles (six km) from Sarehole and Mabel Tolkien could not afford the daily train fare, another move was necessary. From

Birmingham's outer boundaries, the Tolkien trio moved into the city. Ronald hated to leave the trees and countryside he had grown to love. The rural climate had helped develop his slender frame and give a healthy glow to his fair cheeks. Although Ronald had spent only four years in the Sarehole cottage, he recalled those years as "the longest-seeming and most formative part of my life." In a word, Ronald found the family's new house in the Birmingham suburb of Moseley dreadful.

Other big changes took place as well. Mabel Tolkien found her Christian faith a source of strength after her husband's death. She and her sons had been attending Anglican church services, but Mabel eventually turned to Catholicism and took instruction to become a Catholic. Many members of her Protestant family disapproved, but Mabel stood firm. And she shared the new religious instruction with her two sons.

King Edward's School was a large, Gothic building. Its high, carved walls and deep-set windows were covered with heavy black soot. Inside, the school echoed with the noise of students and the constant whistling of nearby railway engines. On old wooden benches, hundreds of youthful scholars recited their Latin and memorized equations. Within the gloomy surroundings, young minds flourished, and graduates of King Edward's often entered England's finest universities.

But John Ronald Reuel Tolkien got off to a slow start. He was not used to the hustle and bustle of noisy, crowded classrooms. His classmates competed fiercely for high grades. Accustomed to his mother's personal encouragement, Ronald did not fare well at King Edward's.

Soon after settling into their new home, the Tolkiens had to move again. Their house was going to be torn down to make room for a fire station. Ronald was delighted to leave. Mabel Tolkien found a larger house, a compact villa (a detached, city residence with yard and garden space) behind King's Heath Station. The back of the house faced a railroad line, and the new house was close to the home of Mabel's parents.

The new location opened another world to Ronald Tolkien. Behind the house, trains rumbled by, shaking everything in the house. Engine whistles blew at all hours; steam hissed from the engines. Trucks rolled into a nearby coal yard, and Ronald could hear the sounds of people at work. Many of the coal trucks bore labels on their sides— Welsh words, such as *Gwalia, Vanasour,* and *Rhonabwy.* What did the words mean? Ronald had no idea. Nor could he pronounce them. But they looked fascinating.

While Ronald found himself caught up in a new world of words, his mother explored her own new world of religion. Because Mabel Tolkien took her new Catholic faith seriously, she wanted her sons to receive religious training at school. Early in 1902, when Ronald was 10 and Hilary was 8, she enrolled them in St. Phillip's Catholic School.

Ronald quickly became bored at St. Phillip's. Despite his many absences at King Edward's, he was still far ahead of his classmates at St. Phillip's. Because of Mabel's decision to convert to Catholicism, her family refused to help her financially. Mabel tutored her two sons, hoping they might qualify for scholarships at King Edward's if she could get them back in. Her efforts paid off. In the fall of 1903, Ronald was back at King Edward's. This time he was determined to stay.

Ronald was placed in the sixth class at King Edward's, a middle grade in a school that combined elementary school

King Edward's School in Birmingham was designed by architect Charles Barry, who also designed both houses of Parliament.

The headmaster's desk, with the word Sapientia *inscribed over it and a rail surrounding it, stands at the front of this classroom. Boards listing the honor roll students hang on the wall to the right.*

and high school. Ronald, along with the other sixth class students, began studying Greek, and yet another world of words opened to Ronald. He immediately liked the language. It flowed so smoothly, yet was "punctuated by hardness." Its ancient origin held a special mystique for a 10-year-old boy.

One of Ronald's teachers, George Brewerton, piqued the interest of his students. He did not just instruct—he performed. He made every lesson a journey into the past to discover the excitement and beauty of words. Brewerton demanded careful listening and quick thinking on the part of his students. Ronald Tolkien, sitting on his wooden bench and listening to every sound, delivered both.

One morning, as Ronald sat poised on his bench, his teacher began another adventure. With a bouncing beat and energy to spare, Brewerton began reading Geoffrey Chaucer's *Canterbury Tales*, probably the most outstanding literary work in Middle English (the form of English used from the 12th to the 15th centuries):

> Whan that Aprill with his shoures soote
> The droghte of Marche hath perced to the roote,
> And bathed every veyne in swich licour
> Of which vertu engendred is the flour...

Pausing, the schoolmaster translated the Middle English into modern terms for the puzzled students. Ronald listened carefully:

> When April with its sweet showers
> The drought of March has pierced to the root,
> And bathed every vein [of earth] in such liquid
> From whose virtue [power] the flower is engendered...

In *Canterbury Tales*, Chaucer describes the lives of various individuals from English society. Their words and actions are vivid and reveal much about their characters. Ronald Tolkien consumed each Chaucer story as if it were a delicious feast. He enjoyed every word as a tasty morsel. Chaucer provided much frank and candid detail in his writing, and schoolmaster Brewerton appreciated Chaucer's style. Brewerton wanted his students to write with a similar freedom and openness and to avoid stiff, stilted usage. He encouraged his students to use plain words, to call a thing what it is rather than refine the term.

At Christmas in 1903, Mabel Tolkien wrote to relatives and boasted about her oldest son's exceptional progress at school. She admitted that he knew far more Greek than she did Latin. She boasted of his First Communion with equal pride.

The new year opened with measles and whooping cough infesting the Tolkien house. Nursing her two sons back to health weakened Mabel, and by April she was in the hospital. The doctor diagnosed diabetes and recommended a long rest. Insulin treatment was not available then.

Father Francis Morgan, a new family friend who was a Catholic priest, offered a solution. He found the Tolkiens rooms in Woodside Cottage on the grounds of the Oratory clergy, a religious order. The rest of the cottage was occupied by the local postman and his wife. There, in the cottage in Rednal, a Worcestershire hamlet near Birmingham, Mabel Tolkien fought to regain her health. The postman's wife even provided meals. During the summer, Ronald and Hilary explored the nearby woods, climbed trees, and raced along the paths and hillsides.

Ronald returned to King Edward's when the school term started in the fall. Each morning he got up while it was still dark, walked a mile to the train station, and rode into Birmingham. Hilary remained at home. He met his older brother with a lantern when Ronald returned after school, again in the dark.

Mabel Tolkien's health weakened even more that fall. In early November, she collapsed on the kitchen floor. Carried to her bed, she sank into a diabetic coma. She lingered in that condition for six days. Then, on November 14, 1904, she died. At the age of 12, John Reuel Ronald Tolkien was suddenly an orphan. He stood with his younger brother at their mother's bedside. The boys gazed sadly and lovingly at the woman who lay peacefully before them. The two boys must have felt empty and alone.

three

EXCITING DISCOVERIES

There was little time for mourning, and Father Francis Morgan knew it. He also knew exactly why Mabel Tolkien had named him executor of her estate and guardian of her two sons. Mabel wanted Ronald and Hilary to be raised in the Catholic faith. Most of the Suffields and Tolkiens probably would not have agreed to raise the boys as Catholics, but Beatrice Suffield, a sister-in-law of Mabel's, had no particular religious feelings. Not only that, she also had a room available in her home. Father Morgan quickly arranged to house Ronald and Hilary with their aunt.

Hilary adjusted readily to the new surroundings. He paid little attention to "Aunt Bea," and she paid little attention to her nephews. Board and lodging was what the arrangement called for, and that is what Aunt Bea provided. Poor and recently widowed, she showed little affection for Ronald and Hilary.

It was Ronald who sorely missed the warm feelings of the past. Often he stood at the window of the top-floor bedroom and looked out on a seemingly endless network of rooftops stretching toward distant factory chimneys. Slivers of green countryside could barely be seen. Ronald felt as if he were in prison. Hilary passed the time by tossing stones at cats in the streets below.

From the nearby Oratory house and its wooded grounds, Father Morgan kept a close watch over the boys. He saw that they were well fed and properly clothed. He dipped into his own pocket to add to the modest funds Mabel Tolkien had left to care for the boys. Each morning Ronald and Hilary hurried from their sleeping quarters at Aunt Bea's, slipped into altar-boy robes, and served Mass for Father Morgan. After a quick breakfast, they headed off to school at King Edward's. If they were early, the boys walked. If they were running late, they caught a horsecar (a streetcar pulled by horses).

Christopher Wiseman, the son of a Methodist minister, became a close friend of Ronald's. Wiseman challenged Ronald in the classroom as well as on the rugby field. From the moment they met in the autumn of 1905, the two boys were constant companions. Their discussions about Latin and Greek lasted for hours, and they enjoyed arguing about religion too. Their minds became well-tuned instruments, able to sift through difficult issues and turn out organized thoughts.

The curriculum at King Edward's revolved around the study of Latin and Greek. While Ronald's classmates often struggled with pronunciations and meanings, Ronald welcomed each new lesson.

Shortly before his 16th birthday, Ronald entered the first (or senior) class at King Edward's. As a senior, he looked

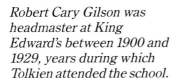

Robert Cary Gilson was headmaster at King Edward's between 1900 and 1929, years during which Tolkien attended the school.

forward to working with Robert Cary Gilson, the headmaster of the school. Gilson was known for more than being an outstanding teacher. He was an inventor too. Some boys talked about how he managed to provide electric light for his whole house by operating a small windmill. Others talked about how the headmaster had constructed the hectograph machine that duplicated exam papers.

An inventor, a scientist, and a classical scholar, Robert Cary Gilson filled many roles. He pushed his students to ask why and how things happened. It was not enough to memorize facts or learn answers. The *process* of learning was important too. Gilson was a master teacher. His students were taught to use his approach whether they were trying to understand machines, the law, or the fine arts.

Two views of King Edward's. The top photo shows the stairway used by the students.

Few expended more energy in learning than Ronald Tolkien. He charged, like a dauntless soldier, into philology, the study of language—including the grammar, forms, sounds of speech, and meanings of words. When did the Latin verb *venire* (to come) first appear? Why was it originated? By whom? How? And what about the Greek noun *phobos* (fear)? What of its history? Its use? The student became a detective, searching, investigating. One clue led to another until—slowly—answers came.

But Ronald's fun with words did not stem only from the pages of books. His cousins Mary and Marjorie Incledon had created their own language out of animal names. They called it *Animalic*, and whenever Ronald visited his relatives at Barnt Green outside Birmingham, he joined the fun. When Marjorie tired of the exchange, Mary and Ronald made up their own language and called it *Nivbosh*, or New Nonsense. It was light and silly, but the two cousins laughed for hours at their own word inventions.

Immersed in Latin and Greek, Ronald met a new challenge through his former instructor George Brewerton. Remembering Tolkien's interest in Chaucer, Brewerton offered the budding philologist an Anglo-Saxon (or Old English) primer. The book introduced Ronald to words used by the English before the Norman conquerors entered England nine centuries earlier. This was history—living, powerful history. Anglo-Saxon was a strong and forceful language. Ronald also discovered the Old English poem *Beowulf*, a magnificent tale of a warrior who fought against two monsters and a dragon. Ronald enjoyed the adventure in the original Old English form and in modern English.

Following Old English, Ronald continued the trail into Middle English, a more recent form of the language. He met

Sir Gawain and the Green Knight, a noble tale of one of King Arthur's finest knights, who set out to find a mysterious giant. The story thrilled young Tolkien.

From Old and Middle English, Ronald leaped into Old Norse. The Scandinavian language revealed an entirely new collection of word sounds and meanings. Years ago he had enjoyed the adventures of Sigurd slaying the dragon Fafnir in *The Red Fairy Book.* Now he read the story in its original language. As a boy, Ronald longed to have the courage of Sigurd and dreamed of killing dragons of his own. For the time being, at least he could enjoy the words of the story and the grandeur of the tale. Memorizing words and phrases, Ronald pored over the book's pages for hours.

When Ronald discovered Cornish's Bookstore down the road from King Edward's, he may have felt like a second Christopher Columbus. From the outside, it was nothing but a drab, dreary storefront like so many others. But on the dusty shelves inside, Ronald found books written in Greek, Latin, Anglo-Saxon, Old Norse, and German. With each book a new mystery unfolded.

Father Morgan encouraged Ronald's interest in languages, but the boy's frequent requests to learn Spanish went unanswered. The clergyman spoke the language fluently, but his schedule was full with church duties and he had little time to spare. Tolkien did use his library and books though, devouring the collection of Spanish texts with hearty appetite.

It was not that Father Morgan ignored his job as guardian to both Ronald and Hilary. Each summer he took them on vacation to Lyme Regis. The bay-side town offered Ronald places to roam and sketch, especially on wet mornings when the fog cloaked the nearby cliffs. The area begged to be explored.

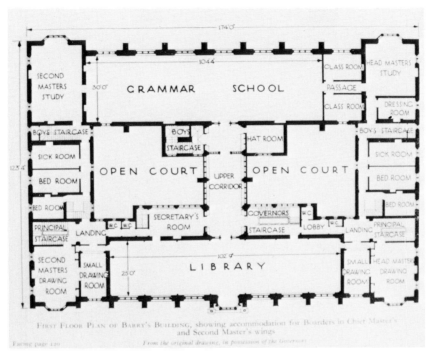

The first-floor plan of King Edward's School

One day as the fog slowly lifted, Ronald strolled along the quiet shore. Sometimes he liked being by himself, remembering the past and daydreaming about the future. Suddenly his eyes widened. Ahead of him lay a strange piece of bone. It was too big to be a human bone. Quickly he ran forward to investigate. By the end of the day, Ronald declared it to be a prehistoric jawbone—probably a piece of petrified dragon. He undoubtedly felt proud of himself.

The holidays at Lyme Regis gave the two boys a chance to tell Father Morgan about how unhappy they were at their Aunt Beatrice's. Father Morgan promised to look for a better place for them in Birmingham.

four

school days

In the spring of 1908, Ronald and Hilary moved to 37 Duchess Road, a boardinghouse run by a Mrs. Faulkner. The new quarters rested peacefully behind the Oratory grounds. The new landlady wore a ready smile, a welcome change from solemn Aunt Beatrice.

Yet it was not Mrs. Faulkner who would have a great influence on the life of 16-year-old Ronald Tolkien. It was the small, slender 19-year-old girl who lived directly below Ronald and Hilary. Her name was Edith Bratt.

The more time Ronald Tolkien spent with Edith, the more he liked her. Although Edith was 19, she was small and slender and did not seem to be three years older than Ronald.

Like Ronald and Hilary, Edith was an orphan. She was musically talented and played the piano very well. She hoped to become a piano teacher or perhaps a concert pianist someday. But for the time being, her guardian had placed her with Mrs. Faulkner, who was fond of music. The landlady enjoyed entertaining guests and was happy to have Edith play the piano to accompany soloists at her social gatherings. But Edith had little chance to practice on her own. As soon as the young girl began playing a few scales, Mrs. Faulkner would hurry into the room and tell Edith to stop. Mrs. Faulkner clearly preferred a quiet house when company was not around. Her dark hair framed her saddened features as Edith retreated to her room.

Ronald could have been shy around Edith. After all, he had had little association with girls his own age. But he wasn't at all shy. Edith listened to him talk about languages and the history of words. Her own education was limited and centered around music, but she appeared eager to learn. They chuckled about "the old lady," their nickname for Mrs. Faulkner, and coaxed the maid to smuggle snacks from the kitchen for them.

Although Edith spent most of her time in her room with her sewing machine, one day Ronald invited her to visit a local tea shop, a type of restaurant. They sat on an upper balcony above the sidewalk, where people were strolling. "I wonder . . . ," Ronald said, a smile spreading across his face. He lifted a lump of sugar from the bowl on the table. Plop! The sugar cube landed neatly on a hat passing below. Ronald enjoyed playing mischievous pranks. Edith could not hide her giggles. Her gray eyes twinkled, and soon she, too, was dropping lumps of sugar onto passing hats. It was great fun!

School offered more excitement as Ronald approached his last years at King Edward's. He studied words and languages more intensely, and he won a place in the debating society, despite a somewhat squeaky voice. With determi-

Rugby is simlilar to football, but in rugby, time-outs, substitutions, interference, and forward passing are not permitted.

nation and force, he defended the goals and actions of supporters of women's rights. In other debates, he attacked the background and character of the great English writer William Shakespeare. According to *King Edward's School Chronicle,* the school magazine, Ronald also deplored the historic invasion of Norman tribes into parts of England because of the influence they had had on the English language. During one debate, Tolkien criticized "the influx of polysyllabic barbarities which ousted the more honest if humbler native words." Simply put, the young debater felt the Normans had damaged the entire English language.

When Ronald wasn't flexing his mental might with the debating society, he took his physical talents to the rugby football field. His taut muscles were stretched over a spindly frame, but what Tolkien lacked in physical size, he made up for in energy and enthusiasm. The *Chronicle* describes Ronald

The Municipal Building in Cheltenham, the borough to which Edith moved in 1910

as "A light but hard-working forward who makes up for his lightness by his determined dash. Tackles well, but his kicking is weak."

This was a happy time in Tolkien's life, but it did not last.

Clearly, Ronald and Edith had fallen in love. Hours slipped by quickly when they were together. But the couple had no desire to promote gossip. After all, Ronald was preparing for an Oxford scholarship. In British society in the early 1900s, it was not thought proper for him to be romancing a young lady who was three years older than he was.

Late in the autumn term of 1909, Ronald found himself in big trouble. Word had reached Father Morgan that Ronald and Edith had been seen sharing tea and company in the country. The priest was shocked. If such things were done publicly, what might be happening under Mrs. Faulkner's roof? Father Morgan summoned the nervous Tolkien and told him of his disappointment. Certainly new housing was required. In addition, the relationship had to end!

Because he had great affection for Father Morgan and was grateful for all the priest had done, Ronald agreed to end his relationship with Edith. He threw himself into his studies. After all, the scholarship exam at Oxford was coming up.

Never had Ronald Tolkien studied so hard. By the time he took the Oxford test, he felt ready. He wanted to make his family (none of whom had attended a university) and Father Morgan proud. After the three-day exam was over, Tolkien checked the notice board to find out the results. He had not won an award, but he could try again the following year. Without a cash grant, Tolkien could not afford to attend the university. Feeling depressed, he walked slowly to the railway station.

The year 1910 began on a similar downhill slide. Hilary and Ronald now lived in a new boardinghouse. Ronald and Edith tried to stay apart, but eventually they met and took a train ride into the countryside. At a jeweler's shop, they bought and exchanged gifts. Ronald bought Edith a watch for her upcoming 21st birthday. She purchased a pen for his 18th birthday.

Once more Father Morgan heard of their meeting. This time he stood firm—no future meetings, nor could they write to each other. Edith's decision to stay with an elderly couple in Cheltenham eased the situation somewhat, since the borough was about 50 miles (80 km) away. The distance would make it more difficult for them to see each other.

It was not a happy prospect, but Ronald accepted it. Eventually Father Morgan agreed to correspondence between the two young people, but the priest insisted that Ronald direct his energies toward school.

Ronald did just that. He took the role of being a member of the first class (the senior class), seriously. He prepared a lecture entitled "The Modern Languages of Europe— Derivations and Capabilities." It took Tolkien three hours just to cover the "derivations." The schoolmaster stopped him before he could present the "capabilities." His classmates were equally astounded when Ronald delivered speeches entirely in Latin, Greek, or Anglo-Saxon.

Rugby captured a good share of his time too. One grueling contest left him with a broken nose, another with a cut tongue. Other boys might have quit, but not Ronald. He was often drawn to the sports field. After the games, he pedaled seven miles (11 km) home, an oil lamp bouncing on the back of his bicycle.

By December of 1910, Ronald Tolkien was again headed to Oxford to take the entrance exam. No doubt, he could have studied more, but he felt confident this time. On December 17, he learned that he had won a scholarship. It was not a lot—£60 a year (about $105)—but with funds available through King Edward's and with Father Morgan's help, Ronald could afford to go to Oxford University.

His future set, Ronald returned to his final months at King Edward's. His classmates elected him secretary of the debating society and football secretary too. He also became a prefect, or school monitor. With a few other seniors, including Christopher Wiseman and the headmaster's son, R. Q. Gilson, Ronald helped run the school library. They called their group the Tea Club.

King Edward's School Chronicle.

DEBATING SOCIETY

The first Debate of the Session was held on Friday, October 8th. Mr. Reynolds took the chair, and D.G.J. Macswiney brought forth the motion: "That this house express its sympathy with the objects and its admiration of the tactics of the Militant Suffragette." Women, he said, did not claim universal franchise, but only that sex should be no disqualification in the case of tax-payers. He then drew a pathetic picture of "drunken wretches grovelling in the gutter six nights out of seven," to prove that many men were less worthy of the vote than women. Peaceable methods had been used for forty years without success, and therefore more violent tactics must be used.

A.B. Harrower, who opposed, poured forth the vials of his indignation upon these "Bacchanalian extravagances." To prove his knowledge of the subject, he mentioned that he had bought three Suffragist pamphlets, of which he had read one and lost the others. Woman was naturally a subordinate creature, and the majority did not want the vote.

R.B. Naish did not agree with the Honourable Opener in some points, but was anxious to avoid all appearance of a split on the Affirmative. The question of the vote only became vital in the case of the women of the lower classes, who were unprotected by trades-unionism. C.L. Wiseman pointed out that man had been educated from the middle of the 18th century, but it was not till 1884 that the vote was extended. Woman had had no education till the middle of the 19th century; ergo, they had still fifty years to wait!

F. Scopes argued that the exercise of the vote has an important educative value. He denied the majority of women did not want the vote, and showed that as women were capable of good judgment in municipal affairs, so they would be in those of the nation.

J.R.R. Tolkien (maiden) spoke of the Suffragette from a Zoological point of view and gave an interesting display of his paronomasiac powers. A good humourous speech.

After the Honourable Opener had replied, the House divided, the votes being: Affirmative 12; Negative 20. The motion was therefore lost.

This excerpt from the November 1909 issue of King Edward's School Chronicle *reports on the debate positions of J.R.R. Tolkien and his friend Christopher Wiseman.*

Outside the gate of Exeter College, Oxford University

The Tea Club—or T.C., as its members called it—gave the group a chance to share jokes and conversation while sipping hot tea in the late afternoon, an old British custom. The T.C. provided rest and relaxation, yet the dialogue was always stimulating. The boys felt grown-up, often mimicking their schoolmasters and telling bawdy stories. When summer came, the Tea Club moved its meetings to the tea room in nearby Barrow's Stores, and the name of the club became T.C.B.S. Its membership grew too and included many seniors who enjoyed books and cheerful chatter. Ronald impressed his audience by reciting from such classics as *Beowulf, The Pearl,* and *Sir Gawain and the Green Knight.* Tolkien's eyes sparkled from the applause and praise as he doubled his slender frame over in a hammy, exaggerated bow. The compliments that he received certainly pleased him, but Ronald sometimes enjoyed being a clown.

In the summer of 1911, the seniors took their final exams at King Edward's. Some were eager to get out. Others feared the thought of being on their own. King Edward's had offered security to Ronald Tolkien. He had made friends with whom he shared laughter and pranks as well as the high and low points of growing up. Soon he would leave all this to begin a new life at Oxford.

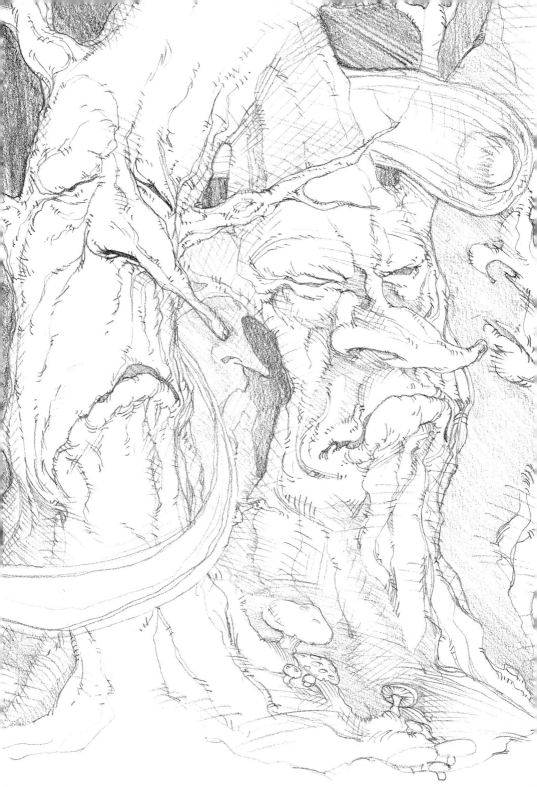

a spark ignites

In the early 1900s, most of the students attending Oxford University came from rich, aristocratic families. But Ronald Tolkien was not among that privileged group. His family background was middle-class at best, and his bills were to be paid from scholarships and financial aid. Most of his classmates at Exeter, one of the 35 colleges that make up Oxford University, were in similar situations. Each shilling and pound was spent carefully.

Ronald arrived at Oxford in an automobile owned and driven by one of his former schoolmasters at King Edward's. R. W. Reynolds, affectionately nicknamed "Dickie" by his pupils, eased the vehicle to a stop on narrow Turl Street. Seeing his name printed in black letters on a board at the foot of a staircase made Ronald feel immediately at home. After climbing the uneven wooden staircase with a broad

45

black banister, he reached his new living quarters—a bedroom and a sitting room. There was nothing fancy about the place, and yet in the eyes of Ronald Tolkien, everything was perfect. He was on his own, and he relished the feeling! Earlier fears and worries slipped silently away.

Exeter boasted a variety of activities for newcomers. Tolkien eagerly signed up for the college essay club and the dialectical society, a formal discussion group. He also played rugby. Just for fun, he started an organization called the Apolausticks. Most of the members were other freshmen. They sat around for hours talking about any topic that a member brought up. Now, regularly puffing on a pipe and parting his hair neatly in the center, Tolkien thought of himself as quite an intellectual.

Students at Oxford and residents of the town of Oxford often found themselves at odds, and Ronald did not have to be coaxed to join the pranks on one particular evening. When the sounds of voices outside drew Ronald and his friends from their rooms, the young men spilled into the street, and a crowd began to form. Shouts and cheers filled the air. What was the cause? As the crowd swelled, no one seemed to know or care. Tolkien and a buddy leaped aboard an empty bus that was nearby. Hooting and honking every block of the way, they drove off, stopping now and then to pick up other students. Thoroughly enjoying the wild prank, Tolkien even made a few speeches to the unruly crowd. Within a few hours the pranks were over, and all the Oxford students were back to their rooms. No disciplinary action was taken, probably because so many people were involved and no damage resulted.

Unfortunately for Ronald, life inside the Exeter classrooms failed to equal the excitement found outside. Preferring to relax with friends, he had to force himself to study for some classes in which dull instructors presented even duller lectures. However, one instructor, Joseph Wright, sparked Tolkien's imagination.

From age six, Wright had worked in a woolen mill. No laws at that time protected children against unfair working conditions. Nor did laws guarantee that children automatically received an education. By the time he reached his teens, Wright wanted to read and write. Slowly he taught himself, and soon he was teaching others. Wanting to learn more, he went to night school to study French and German. When he was 21, he traveled to Germany. At Heidelberg University, he became even more interested in languages. Whether it was Old English or Russian, Gothic or Old Saxon, Wright could not get enough. After he earned a doctorate, he returned to England and took a teaching job at Oxford. He also started writing dictionaries and language books.

In Joe Wright, Ronald Tolkien discovered not only a fine teacher but a role model. Soon Ronald filled not only a desk in Wright's classroom but also a place at the Wright family's dining room table. Over giant slices of plum cake, the eager student listened to his professor talk about ancient Greek.

Thanks to Wright, Tolkien's spark of interest in the Welsh language became a blazing bonfire. Both men thought it was a language with beauty in both its sound and its appearance.

During the Christmas holiday of 1911, Tolkien returned to Birmingham. His old school chums at King Edward's invited him to take part in the T.C.B.S. performance of an 18th-century play by Richard Brinsley Sheridan called *The Rivals*. Tolkien willingly accepted. His role was that of Mrs. Malaprop, a woman known for her humorous misuse of words.

During the summer vacation of 1912, Tolkien spent two weeks at a camp with a cavalry regiment he had joined. It

The front quad and the chapel at Exeter, the college Tolkien attended at Oxford University

was fun riding horses over the plains of Kent, a county in the southeastern part of England, but he hated the cold, wet nights. When the camp ended, Tolkien took a vacation in Berkshire, where he walked the British countryside and sketched the scenes he enjoyed. He resigned from the regiment a few months later.

When he went back to school, a new discovery awaited him: a Finnish grammar book opened up a whole new world of language to him. In studying Finnish poems, Tolkien was fascinated with the vast realm of mythology, its gods and goddesses, heroes, heroines, and villains. The stories held mystery and drama, romance and adventure. Why had such literature been forgotten? Why was it so seldom found or read? Tolkien knew that the same thing had happened to many of the ballads and tales of other cultures. So much had seemingly disappeared.

Tolkien had thoughts of creating a British mythology, but those thoughts were quickly swept aside. There were papers to write for his classes at Exeter. The essay club members wanted to hear his writing efforts. There were letters to write home, too, and he even wrote a play for his Incledon relatives at Barnt Green, where he spent Christmas in 1912.

At midnight on January 3, 1913, Ronald celebrated his 21st birthday. He used the occasion to express once more his love to Edith Bratt in a letter. Of legal age, he could now marry.

Edith's reply came as a bombshell. Doubting Ronald's continued interest in her, Edith had found another boyfriend. She was engaged to someone named George Field.

Saddened and dismayed, Ronald read her letter again and again. Edith may have written that she was engaged, but

The Exeter College group, 1912

she did not sound happy about it. Not only did Tolkien know and understand words, he could also sense the feelings behind them. Edith was not convincing. With determination to win her back, Ronald Tolkien boarded a train to Cheltenham, where Edith met him. By the end of the day, her engagement to George Field was broken. Ronald Tolkien had won Edith back. Returning to school, Ronald wrote to Father Morgan about Edith. Although the priest was far from pleased, he accepted his ward's decision.

Next, Tolkien threw himself into his studies. Important tests were coming up, but he had spent too much time visiting with friends long into the night. Tolkien hastily threw papers and reports together. They were far from Tolkien's best efforts. He knew it too. When he received a second class result (similar to receiving a B), Tolkien sighed with relief. He had been lucky to do that well, yet he knew he should have been at the first class level. Because his top score was in philology, Tolkien decided to concentrate on that subject. He transferred to the Oxford Honor School of English Language and Literature.

Now Tolkien felt his life was taking definite direction. If they were to be married, Edith would have to become a Catholic. She agreed and began taking instruction.

It was also essential that Tolkien finish school and find a job. Schoolwork demanded more attention, since the Oxford Honor School of English Language and Literature set high standards. There were no shortcuts to success, no quick ways to score high marks. Professors demanded quality reports and projects, and classroom discussions were intense. With renewed spirit, Tolkien tackled his assignments.

In studying one old Anglo-Saxon poem, Tolkien became intrigued by two lines, which he read again and again.

Eala Earendel engla beorhtast
ofer middangeard monnum sended.

To most people, the lines meant nothing, but to Tolkien, a scholar of words, the meaning was clear.

Hail Earendel, brightest of angels
above the middle-earth sent unto men.

Who was Earendel? Maybe it was John the Baptist, if one viewed it in a spiritual sense. Or perhaps it was Venus, if one accepted a mythological or astronomical meaning. Whoever or whatever it was, the lines had a deep effect on Tolkien. Something stirred within him and awakened a strange sensation. He felt a curious thrill, as if he could grasp meanings and feelings from the past.

SIX

shadows of war

Life brightened for Ronald Tolkien early in 1914. On January 8, exactly a year after their reunion, Edith became a Catholic. Soon afterward they announced their engagement.

Tolkien fixed up his rooms at Exeter too. He bought new furniture and put Japanese prints on his walls. He visited the tailor and purchased two new suits. The changes gave him a feeling of style, of comfort with himself and his surroundings.

The college debating society elected him president. He also captured the Skeat Prize for English, a cash award that Tolkien promptly spent on books.

Visits to Warwick, where Edith was staying with a cousin, offered escape from campus pressures, and short vacations gave him a chance to sketch. During long walks, he soaked in the sights and sounds of nature. In 1914 he took a trip to Cornwall, a county along the sea in the southwestern part of England.

Scenes from Warwick, above, *where Ronald Tolkien often went to visit with Edith*

On his 1914 trip, Tolkien enjoyed the beauty of the seascapes in Cornwall, England, above.

Clear, crisp images filled Tolkien's mind. Words that were once forceful standing alone gained even greater strength tied together in visually descriptive phrases. Reflecting on a line studied earlier about Earendel, Tolkien wrote his own poem about a mythical starship. In the poem, Earendel captains the vessel. Tolkien called the poem "The Voyage of Earendel the Evening Star," and it begins like this:

> Earendel sprang up from the Ocean's cup
> In the gloom of the mid-world's rim;
> From the door of the Night as a ray of light
> Leapt over the twilight brim,
> And launching his bark like a silver spark
> From the golden-fading sand
> Down the sunlit breath of Day's fiery death
> He sped from Westerland.

Earendel's night ride continues until dawn's light ends the voyage. Tolkien was pleased with the effort, but he had no thought of using it again.

While Tolkien's own world gained direction and purpose, the outside world grew more unstable. By the late summer of 1914, England had declared war on Germany. Thousands of men signed up to join the British war effort. Hilary Tolkien was one of them, but Ronald was determined to finish his studies at Oxford. News that students could get army training while still at school cheered him. Ronald signed up, willing to serve his country immediately after he completed work on his degree.

Tolkien thrived on activity—writing poems, going to classes, drilling with the training corps, traveling to see Edith, visiting with friends—and he seldom tired. In the midst of all these activities, he began to make up another language. By 1915, the new language, influenced by Finnish

This was the scene at the Central Recruiting Office in Great Scotland Yard in August 1914. By September 5, more than 250,000 men had volunteered for service in World War I.

words and phrases, was taking a form of its own. Tolkien spent hours creating poems and stories with the new words.

Tolkien felt confident when he took his final exams. Sure enough, his scores earned him first class honors. He thought that there would be little trouble getting a teaching job after his war duties were over.

The new Oxford graduate became a second lieutenant in a British regiment called the Lancashire Fusiliers. He was assigned to drill incoming soldiers. Always looking younger than his age, Ronald grew a moustache to appear older. On weekends, he jumped on a motorbike and visited Edith in nearby Warwick.

The war routine bored Tolkien. He fought to stay awake in lectures and disliked leading the repetitious, monotonous

British soldiers of World War I march along the Strand, one of London's oldest and busiest streets.

drills. The meals were inedible. There was nothing enjoyable about activities focused on "the art of killing."

Happier moments arrived when Tolkien got the chance to learn signals. He quickly mastered Morse and other codes. Waving signal flags and shooting signal rockets enlivened the daily schedule. Signals befitted a lover of communication more readily than drilling did. He spent hours practicing flag signals, light signals, and even the use of carrier pigeons as messengers.

Tolkien knew he would be heading to France. Whether he would come back was another question. Each day brought more names of soldiers killed in action. Whatever happened, he knew he wanted one dream fulfilled before he sailed. On March 22, 1916, Edith Bratt became Edith Tolkien. She was 27; he was 24.

Ronald found Edith a place to stay near his army post. She was just settled in when he received orders to embark for France. It was a sad parting for the newlyweds, but they had expected it.

Early in June 1916, Tolkien headed for London and then on to France. There was some comfort in knowing his school friends from King Edward's were still a part of his life. Chris Wiseman was in the navy, while Rob (R. Q.) Gilson and G. B. Smith, another friend from T.C.B.S., were in the army. They kept in contact through letters, bolstering each other's spirits and remembering the good times of the past. In his T.C.B.S. days, Ronald and his friends had shared exciting dreams of someday writing grand tales of brave warriors and evil villains. What a happy adventure that would be!

But there was little happiness for Ronald Tolkien as he trudged across the French countryside. Most marches took place at night so the British soldiers couldn't be seen by the enemy. During training drills, the soldiers had used perfect equipment under ideal conditions. Field telephones had jangled loud and clear, men had run along smooth pathways, weapons had sparkled in the sunlight. It had been playacting, a game. Now, on the war front, loose wires hung from poles, phones were out of order, roads were blocked or blown away, uniforms and guns were covered with mud and grime.

And then there were the bodies—the torn remainders of men—in trenches and on battlefields. Some of the soldiers were older than Tolkien, but others were years younger. Lives barely begun now lay destroyed. Tolkien described trench warfare as "animal horror."

Days crept into weeks as Tolkien's regiment attacked German soldiers in trenches. Was it a victory? A defeat? No one ever really knew. After each attack, there would be a brief time for rest. Then it would start again. There was little joy in battle.

Most young men thought going off to war would be a great adventure, but they soon learned how terrible it was. Out of every 100 soldiers who fought, 63 were killed.

In France, soldiers fought battles from the trenches, amidst the stench of urine, feces, and decaying flesh from dead bodies.

In July, the weary soldier Tolkien received sad news. G. B. Smith wrote that Rob Gilson had been killed. Memories of their many happy years at King Edward's came back to Tolkien. Tolkien felt that the T.C.B.S. had ended, but Smith immediately rejected that thought. In August, Tolkien met Smith. They shared conversation and a meal. Nearby, bombs exploded.

Although Tolkien had managed to escape any war injury, the dreaded "trench fever" caught up with him in October. Carried by lice, the ailment brought a high temperature and dizziness. With treatment, most soldiers recovered in about a week or two, but not Tolkien. When his fever persisted, he was transported back to a hospital in Birmingham, England. Edith hurried to the hospital to look after him.

By mid-December, when Ronald Tolkien was ready to leave the hospital and go home, a letter from Christopher Wiseman brought a sadness and pain greater than any physical suffering. G. B. Smith was dead. He had been killed on December 3rd.

Again, memories of the hopes and dreams of the T.C.B.S. members flooded Tolkien's mind. They were going to do great things. How strong their friendship had been! Now death had cut into their ranks. Tolkien felt empty, alone.

But another feeling also took root—a need to create. It was true enough that death could claim even the young and strong. Tolkien had seen that clearly. Yet words, thoughts, ideas—carefully chosen—could endure. They could have a lifetime of their own. That thought gave Tolkien a fresh desire to go on.

seven

answering a challenge

In 1917 Ronald Tolkien began putting together the pieces of a puzzle. As he left the military hospital with Edith, Ronald knew what he wanted to do. He would create a literary masterpiece, no matter how long it would take.

Why? Perhaps it was because Tolkien longed to give England a gift, a special kind of present. He loved his country, and England did not have its own rich mythology. He remembered reading *The Kalevala*, a wonderful collection of poems that captured the mystery and drama of the people and gods of Finland. If Finland could have a rich collection of grand, heroic tales, shouldn't England also have one?

What a challenge it would be to create new words, characters, places, and events. In the past, Ronald had created languages merely for fun. Tolkien had already written poetry, and some of it had even been published. Memories of his years at King Edward's returned, of the T.C.B.S., where he had won smiles and cheers with some of his poems. Other poems had triggered serious discussion. Never would Ronald be able to share those moments at school with Chris, Rob, and G.B.S. again, but he would always remember them.

Maybe the spirit of the past could be reborn. Ronald had thought about putting together a long literary work, but the thought had not stayed with him for long. Then Ronald received a note from Chris Wiseman saying, "You ought to start the epic." Did the navy man know Ronald's thinking? Could Tolkien ignore such prodding? Hardly.

Edith brought Ronald from the hospital to Great Haywood, a village not far from his army post. Within days, the recovering soldier began "The Book of Lost Tales," the work that would later become known as *The Silmarillion.*

Tolkien had read thousands of legends from many different countries. He knew their structures and contents. Yet he did not want to copy any other story. For England, his own beloved country, he hoped to write with clear and simple beauty.

For his setting, Tolkien recalled the Norse legend of *Midgard.* In early English, the word meant *Middle-earth.* Tolkien chose to place the action in an imaginary period of antiquity. The characters would be elves, dwarves, and orcs (evil goblins). Yet they would be driven by human forces, for Tolkien wanted his legends to be believable. There would be no silliness, no fanciful tricks.

As Tolkien embarked on his task, Edith helped all she could. She copied his writings in a large book. In the evenings they relaxed together. He often sketched while she played the piano.

Tolkien's imagination blossomed with each story. His elves became artists and poets, full of life and energy. Each character had his or her own name, purpose, and goal. Although they resembled human beings in appearance, the characters went untouched by disease or death (unless slain in battle). They had their own language and customs. The task of creating the stories was a challenge Tolkien happily set for himself.

Tolkien wrote every day. He knew that when he was better, he would have to return to his army duties. But just when he seemed to regain his health, his fever would flare up again. He was in and out of hospitals often during 1917. Edith returned to Cheltenham to stay with a cousin. She was pregnant and needed care herself.

On November 17, 1917, Ronald and Edith welcomed their first child into the world. They named him John Francis Reuel Tolkien. After the baby was christened, Tolkien felt well enough to return to his military duties. Edith and the baby stayed in the village of Roos, England, a short distance from the army base. Now that he was a full lieutenant, Tolkien was able to get leave more often. When they were together, he and Edith frequently went for walks in a nearby wood.

Despite his busy schedule, Tolkien continued writing. Most of the stories revolve around the evil power Morgoth and the elves of Gondolin. But Tolkien was also inspired by his love for Edith. His love is expressed in the character Beren, a mortal man who falls in love with the immortal elvish maid Luthien Tinuviel. Luthien was Edith. The story became the favorite of both Ronald and Edith.

As the war days drew to a close, Tolkien kept receiving orders to move to different places. Edith was tired of moving. Even with her cousin Jennie Grove to help, caring for a baby was no easy task. When Tolkien again found himself in the hospital, Edith could not hide her disgust about the amount of bed rest he had had since his return from France. Undoubtedly she found the thought of rest very appealing.

By the fall of 1918, Tolkien was released from the hospital. The end of the war was in sight, and it was time to find a job. Surely, he thought, there was a teaching post available somewhere.

Tolkien returned to Oxford to seek a position. The university had changed greatly since he had been a student there. The war effort had claimed both teachers and students; many never returned home. As Tolkien strolled among the university buildings, he heard the voices of professors lecturing, and visions of old classmates filled his mind. But when Tolkien asked about job openings, the answers were the same.

At each stop, the news was grim. Only William Craigie, Tolkien's teacher of Icelandic, offered a small hope. Craigie was working with the staff of *The New English Dictionary.* Knowing how talented his former student was with words, Craigie offered Tolkien a job working on the project. Tolkien eagerly accepted.

On November 11, 1918, World War I officially came to an end. Tolkien wasted no time in contacting his army superiors. He requested permission to be stationed at Oxford in order to complete his education until he was discharged from military service. The request was granted.

Christmas brought a special merriment to Ronald. He was back at Oxford, living in rooms only a short distance from where he had stayed as a student. But this time he was with Edith and their baby son. The war was over and he had a job, a job working with words. Ronald often laughed as he cradled John Francis in his arms.

The future looked bright.

J.R.R. Tolkien, later in life, at Oxford University

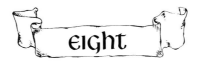

eight

enter a hobbit

A bitter winter wind stung Ronald Tolkien's cheeks as he hurried along Broad Street toward the Old Ashmolean Building. It was only a stone's toss from his living quarters at 50 St. John's Street in Oxford. Once inside, he slipped out of his heavy cloth coat and into a tweed jacket. Lighting his pipe, he joined his fellow lexicographers (authors or editors of dictionaries) working on *The New English Dictionary.*

The dictionary had been started in 1878. Some sections, *A* to *H*, had already been published, but the war had caused delays, and the project still needed work. Tolkien was assigned words beginning with *W*. Was the work dull? Not to Ronald Tolkien. With care and energy, he traced the history and meaning of *warm, water,* and *winter.* Each word was put on a card, and all the cards were neatly sorted. Each day the stack grew.

Tolkien didn't put in a full day at the dictionary workroom. He also tutored university students mostly from the women's colleges of Oxford. Students of ancient languages, these women needed someone to teach them Anglo-Saxon. Since Tolkien was married, he taught them in his home, and no chaperon was required.

By the late summer of 1919, Ronald and Edith could afford to rent a small house. They even hired a cook-housemaid, a special help to Edith, who was pregnant again.

Ronald Tolkien proved a popular tutor. "He's so patient," more than one student noted, and the word spread. Soon he was teaching so much, he could afford to give up his position on the dictionary staff. When he wasn't tutoring, Tolkien sat at a table and added to "The Book of Lost Tales." At night he sometimes read aloud to Edith while she played the piano.

Tolkien accepted an invitation to return to Exeter to read "The Fall of Gondolin." The students present sat spellbound as he shared the battles of heroic elves against the evil Morgoth. At the end, the audience rose, clapping and cheering. A grateful Tolkien bowed deeply. This time he was truly moved by the applause, and his bow was without any silly antics.

During the summer of 1920, Tolkien learned of another job opening. The University of Leeds needed a lecturer and researcher in Anglo-Saxon and Middle English. The post paid well and, with a second child on the way, Tolkien needed the money. He applied for the position and was surprised to get it.

Tolkien rode the train north to Leeds each week and returned to Oxford on weekends. In October Edith gave birth to a second son, who was christened Michael Hilary Reuel Tolkien.

Ronald and Edith did not like being apart so much. Ever since they had married, Tolkien's war duties and jobs had

The Great Hall at the University of Leeds

separated them. Late in 1921 they rented a house in Leeds. It was a small place, but at least their family was together.

In 1922 a young man named Eric Gordon joined the English staff at Leeds. Gordon had known Tolkien while both were at Oxford. In fact Tolkien had tutored Gordon in 1919. Now they worked as writers, putting together a new edition of the Middle English poem *Sir Gawain and the Green Knight*. Tolkien and Gordon offered new notes, interpretations, and a glossary that won quick praise from teachers and struggling university students alike.

Tolkien did not only write books for school use. He also increased his writing of myths and legends, and some of the works appeared in magazines. "The Book of Lost Tales" kept growing. He created a universe for his story. Then he wrote of a craftsman named Feanor and the Silmarils, the beautiful yet deadly jewels stolen by the evil Morgoth. But each time Tolkien came close to completing the story, he stopped to change parts of it. He wanted it to be perfect.

In 1924, at the age of 32, Tolkien was named a full professor at the University of Leeds. Few teachers achieved such a position so young. Ronald and Edith celebrated by buying a house on the outskirts of Leeds. The house was a stately brick structure surrounded by open fields, where the children could play. The timing was perfect. In November a third son, Christopher Reuel Tolkien, was added to the growing family.

As happy as he was at Leeds, Tolkien longed to return to Oxford. In late winter of 1925, he learned there was an opening there. He quickly applied, but because there were three other fine candidates for the job, Tolkien held out little hope for getting it. When he learned that he had been accepted for the position of professor of Anglo-Saxon, he almost dropped the pipe he had been smoking.

Ronald found a house on Northmoor Road in North Oxford that met the family's needs. North Oxford was a community of varied houses, occupied by Oxford professors and their families and servants. In 1926 the Tolkiens moved into a pale brick house that was shaped like an L. It boasted high ceilings, and ivy covered the exterior. Although the Tolkiens moved to a neighboring house on the same street in 1930, they remained on Northmoor Road for 21 years. From there, Ronald bicycled to his classes.

He received a warm welcome from the other teachers at Oxford. Another professor, named C. S. Lewis, became a

C.S. Lewis, author of The Chronicles of Narnia, The Screwtape Letters, *and other books, was a close friend of Tolkien's.*

close friend of Tolkien's. Lewis was a writer too. Together they started writing clubs at which they could read their work aloud. Tolkien welcomed the chance to befriend others with similar interests in language and literature.

But Tolkien's favorite audience was at home. He entertained his eldest son, John, with the adventures of a red-headed boy called Carrots, who climbed into a cuckoo clock. As soon as they were old enough, Michael and Chris begged for stories too. All three boys squealed with laughter over the antics of their father's merry and noble elves and dwarves, but the dreaded dragons and orcs caused the trio to cower under the covers. Always, his sons begged to hear more.

The Tolkien house at 22 Northmoor Road, where the family lived from 1930 until 1947

In 1929, Edith Tolkien again gave birth, this time to a baby girl who was promptly christened Priscilla Mary Reuel. At last Edith had the daughter she had hoped for.

For Ronald Tolkien, yet another birth took place that year. It happened on a July afternoon as he sat grading exam papers in the house on Northmoor Road. Despite the heat, Tolkien wore his usual gray tweed jacket and puffed on his pipe. As he flipped a page over, something happened—one of the students had left a page blank. How empty and alone the page appeared, after so many pages of scribbled, hurried thoughts. It almost begged to be written on. Then a sentence popped suddenly into the teacher's head and he wrote it down: "In a hole in the ground there lived a hobbit."

A "hobbit?" What exactly was a hobbit? In all the languages he had studied, all the words he had read, Tolkien knew he had never come upon the word *hobbit*. He sat back and smiled. This hobbit would bear some further investigation, he decided.

Before long, Tolkien had named his hobbit Bilbo Baggins. Bilbo took on an identity, much like that of Tolkien himself. Bilbo was middle-aged, smoked a pipe, and had few worries.

Tolkien soon decided that he could not have only one hobbit. There had to be more. He visualized the hobbits as being much like rustic English people, just smaller in size. They lacked imagination, yet had plenty of courage.

Tolkien tried out his hobbit tales on his children. Each night they listened as Bilbo traveled through woods and tunnels and faced trolls and dragons—all in a quest for treasure. "More!" John would demand, and his brothers echoed "More!" Tolkien wrote down the adventures he made up during these storytelling sessions. Perhaps, just perhaps, they would be published someday.

The Inklings liked the hobbit tales too. The Inklings were a group of university teachers who gathered to share some of the works they had written. C. S. Lewis was an Inkling, and he applauded Tolkien's efforts.

Sometimes his prose rhymed, sometimes it didn't, but Tolkien always tried to keep his reader or listener anxious to know what would happen next. He also liked making the reader do some of the work. In his writing about literary works, such as *The Odyssey* or *Beowulf*, he did all the explaining. He wanted to make the reader understand everything, to make every point clear. *The Hobbit* was different. With Bilbo Baggins, Tolkien wanted to give readers a chance to create adventures. Tolkien provided a general scheme or outline, but he allowed readers to use their own imaginations.

The White Horse was a pub frequented by the Inklings. It was here that The Lord of the Rings *was first read aloud in 1944.*

Tolkien's work on the story went well until it was about three-quarters done. The dragon Smaug had just been slain. Then Tolkien simply stopped writing. Lewis and other Inkling members kept asking for more adventures, but when the Tolkien boys had outgrown nighttime story sessions, their father had put the uncompleted manuscript aside.

Nevertheless, word of the manuscript leaked out. Elaine Griffiths, one of Tolkien's former students, had gone to work for a London publisher, George Allen & Unwin Ltd. She told people at the publishing company about the adventures of Bilbo Baggins, and one day in 1936 an editor knocked at Tolkien's door. At the end of their visit, the editor carried the manuscript back to London.

Soon a letter from Allen & Unwin arrived at the house on Northmoor Road. The editors liked the story, but what about the ending? By October of 1936, the work was completed.

The final decision to publish the book rested with 10-year-old Rayner Unwin, the son of the publishing company's chairman. When the boy wrote a glowing review, the matter was ended. The manuscript was scheduled for publication.

Always a perfectionist, Tolkien worried about how the book would look and be received. The publishers decided the book needed illustrations and asked to see the drawings Tolkien had done for the story. Eight of the ten illustrations he sent them were accepted. Next, Tolkien had to redo many of the maps for the book, and then he chose to do some rewriting. It never seemed to be just right. He tried not to make too many big changes, so that the printers would not have trouble resetting the type. When he rewrote parts of the book, he used the same number of words that he had used in the original manuscript.

The first copy of *The Hobbit, or There and Back Again* appeared on September 21, 1937. A nervous J. R. R. Tolkien flipped through the pages of the volume. What would people think? he wondered. Just what would they think?

nine

Bilbo and Frodo Triumph

The newspaper reviews of *The Hobbit* poured in quickly. The writing style of the *Times* of London review was very familiar. Tolkien's friend and colleague C. S. Lewis wrote "All who love that kind of children's book which can be read and re-read by adults, should take note that a new star has appeared in the constellation. . . ."

Other reviewers echoed this praise. In a publicity piece, Allen & Unwin compared *The Hobbit* to Lewis Carroll's *Alice in Wonderland*, since both authors were Oxford dons, or teachers. But some reviewers saw definite differences between the two literary efforts. "Carroll created a collection of fascinating characters and fun adventures. Tolkien, on the other hand, offers readers a journey into another world occupied by his own creations of hobbits, wizards, [and] dwarves. . . ." Observed another reviewer, "Tolkien, in his volume *The*

Hobbit, or There and Back Again, has earned the title 'master of fantasy.' Opening the pages of this book is like opening a rich treasure chest. Each word is a sparkling jewel."

Naturally, Tolkien was delighted with the response. He was equally pleased to learn from his publisher that he would likely earn some extra money from the book. With four children, Tolkien often found himself low on funds.

By Christmas of 1937, the first edition of *The Hobbit* had sold out in England. Plans called for the book to be published in the United States the following year. When *The Hobbit* was published by Houghton Mifflin Company in the United States, it again received outstanding reviews. "Although written by an Oxford professor," observed one newspaper reviewer, "the book is an exciting, fun-filled adventure that people everywhere can read with zest. The author is clearly a scholar, but more importantly, he is a writer. He knows how to reach a young person's imagination and hold it, and that young person can be anywhere between five and ninety-five."

Tolkien discovered there was little time to enjoy the praise for his efforts. Already Stanley Unwin, one of his publishers, was asking for a sequel to *The Hobbit*.

Maybe, thought Tolkien, this was the time for publishing the giant collection of myths, legends, and songs he had begun so long ago. Once called "The Book of Lost Tales," it was now called *The Silmarillion*, a title chosen from the three great jewels which form the core of the story's plot. He also had a few short stories for children.

But the manuscripts failed to interest his publishers. They were looking for another hobbit book, and readers everywhere seemed to demand the same thing.

Tolkien thought he had said all he had to say about hobbits. Nonetheless, he agreed to try.

Tolkien tried to introduce a new hobbit in the character of Bilbo's son Bingo Baggins, but that did not suit the author. Instead, Tolkien created Bilbo's nephew Bingo Bolger Baggins, who would find a ring. The ring would provide a connection with *The Hobbit*. Yes, that might work. Tolkien quickly put pen to paper.

Once the story took form, Tolkien sent it to his publishers and requested that young Rayner Unwin again look it over. After all, the boy had been most helpful with the original *Hobbit*. Rayner cheerfully agreed.

But the more Tolkien continued work on the new book, the more it drifted away from the light, happy style of *The Hobbit*. The language of the sequel was more adult, the thoughts on a deeper plane. Ronald lacked the audience he had once had for comment and reaction. All his children were grown now, beyond storytelling age. Weeks drifted into months, months into years. Again and again Tolkien tried to force a story line, but he was never satisfied.

Outside events distracted him as well. His son Christopher developed a heart problem. He was required to stay in bed and needed constant attention. Tolkien and his wife took turns watching over their son, and Christopher slowly regained his strength. It was a joy when Christopher could again join his father in the garden, as the older man fussed and fumed over the latest invasion of weeds. But when Ronald went for long, rambling walks into the country, he strolled by himself, alone with his thoughts.

England's entry into World War II changed the student population at Oxford. Many service cadets flocked to the campus to take "short courses" before taking on officers' duties. Tolkien wrote a minitext for these students and spent time shortening his lectures. This was no easy task since

The plaque below hangs on a wall in this pub, another of the Inklings' gathering spots.

C. S. LEWIS,
his brother, W. H. Lewis, J. R. R. Tolkien,
Charles Williams and other friends
met every Tuesday morning, between
the years 1939-1962 in the back room
of this their favourite pub. These men,
popularly known as the "Inklings", met
here to drink Beer and to discuss,
among other things, the books they
were writing.

Tolkien often presented more than 100 lectures yearly. Responding to the war effort personally, Tolkien volunteered as an air raid warden. Fortunately, Oxford University was spared any direct attacks.

Despite the distractions, Tolkien plugged away at a sequel to *The Hobbit*. He called it *The Lord of the Rings*, and by the end of 1942, he sent word to Stanley Unwin that it was almost finished.

But by the middle of 1943, Tolkien notified his publisher that he was stuck again. No matter how hard he tried, Tolkien seemed unable to complete his writing task. He worked long into the night, and although he always hated waking up early, he did so in order to continue his work. He wanted a map to record the action. The names of the characters had to be perfect, the pace and phrasing crisp and exact. Tolkien would not settle for less, so he continued to struggle with the work.

Christopher Tolkien joined the struggle. A writing enthusiast himself, he was now training as a pilot in South Africa. His father mailed him accounts of the book's progress, and the two exchanged ideas.

Tolkien's old friend C. S. Lewis joined the campaign to get *The Hobbit* sequel finished. Another Inkling and published writer, Charles Williams, became a part of the effort too.

Tolkien appreciated the interest and encouragement, but he knew that it was up to him to get the job done. He continued to produce short scholarly works, but progress on *The Lord of the Rings* was slow. In 1949 Allen & Unwin published a funny Tolkien tale about heroes and dragons called *Farmer Giles of Ham*, and it was published in the United States the following year. For years, Tolkien fans had been told another hobbit book was in the making. With the appearance of *Farmer Giles of Ham*, more people asked, "What about the new hobbit book?"

What about it, indeed? To Tolkien's readers, it might be a *new* hobbit book, but to the author, the task had grown old and tiring. Finally, he devoted himself to finishing the work. In February 1950, after 12 years of work, he wrote to Allen & Unwin to announce that *The Lord of the Rings* was done. The battle to finish the sequel was over.

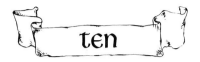

sunset over middle-earth

Tolkien's publishers were happy to learn that *The Lord of the Rings* was finally finished. Yet they were not so interested in publishing *The Silmarillion*, which Tolkien was also eager to see in print. Not only did Tolkien think *The Silmarillion* was a good piece of literature, it also stood as a memorial to the former schoolmates who were killed in World War I. To Tolkien, it was a matter of honor to see it published. But Allen & Unwin did not see it that way.

Unhappy with his publishing house, Tolkien decided to find another. Collins Publishing, a distinguished British firm, showed a quick interest. The only problem was that *The Lord of the Rings* was almost half a million words, and paper expenses were soaring. Collins wanted Tolkien to cut the manuscript—to make the story shorter. Tolkien felt it had already been cut as much as possible. Tolkien also wanted to

The Tolkien residence on Sandfield Road in Headington

do some final work on *The Silmarillion,* and he thought it would end up being half a million words too. Because of paper costs, Collins Publishing backed away from the deal, so Tolkien took his work back to Allen & Unwin. Tolkien agreed to Allen & Unwin's idea of publishing only *The Lord of the Rings.* The publisher was glad to have him back again.

At the same time Tolkien was grappling with his publishing problems, he and Edith were trying to find a suitable home. As the older boys grew up and left home, the house on Northmoor Road began to seem too large for their needs. Since 1945, when he had become Merton Professor of English Language and Literature at Oxford's Merton College, Tolkien had lived in one of the college houses. In 1950 Ronald, Edith, and Priscilla moved into a house on Holywell

J.R.R. Tolkien resting against a tree during a few moments of relaxation

Street, but the traffic there proved too noisy. In the spring of 1953, the Tolkiens bought a house in Headington, just east of Oxford, and moved once again.

New battles raged over the publication of *The Lord of the Rings*. Allen & Unwin simply could not publish the work as one book. It had to be done as three separate volumes. Tolkien insisted that *The Lord of the Rings* remain as the overall title, while the three individual books were to be called *The Fellowship of the Ring, The Two Towers,* and *The Return of the King.*

Tolkien also had to give up other ideas about the design of *The Lord of the Rings*. The publishers could not afford the author's wishes for colored ink for certain letters or a special color process to make the pages of one section look old and burnt. The printers had changed the spelling of certain key words, but Tolkien insisted on retaining his own spelling. He preferred *elven* to *elfin, elvish* to *elfish,* and *dwarves* to *dwarfs.* The maps for the books posed special problems too. However, Christopher Tolkien, who was now a writer and artist, stepped in to help with those.

In August 1954, *The Fellowship of the Ring* appeared. The book was received enthusiastically in the United States as well as in England. "We welcome Frodo Baggins, Tolkien's new hobbit, as we would welcome a prodigal son," wrote one newspaper reviewer. "And we are even more delighted to learn there are more such adventures to come!" Tolkien was pleased that most of the reviews were good. A fan letter from an English boy proved especially amusing. "It is bloody well time you wrote more about hobbits," the young reader wrote. "We have been waiting far too long."

Tolkien promised to supply an index of names for *The Lord of the Rings* series. But as he struggled to complete it, the demand for the other two volumes increased. They were published without Tolkien's index. Soon publishers in foreign countries obtained the publishing rights to the books, and J. R. R. Tolkien became a literary name known all over the world.

Tolkien was flattered by all the attention and fame. Invitations to speak, in England and abroad, poured in. Each day brought letters from readers, most in glowing praise of his work, and gifts came too. The author was pleased people enjoyed his work, yet it was the stories themselves that he felt were important, not the author. "It is the message that is important in literature," Tolkien told his Oxford students as he stood before his classes, "not the messenger." He even

*Tolkien in
his study at
Oxford, 1973*

downplayed the message within his own work and insisted
that he wanted only to entertain his readers, lift their spirits,
and engage them in linguistic games.

In the summer of 1959, the popular university professor
gave his final lecture. He knew it would not be easy to give
up the work he had been doing for 40 years. But time was
catching up with him. His steps had slowed, while his speech
patterns had speeded up, sometimes making it hard for
people to understand his words. Wrinkles now lined the
once-smooth face, and even a tight waistcoat could not hide
the paunchy middle. The days of bicycling to classes lay
behind him.

Edith loved the coastal town of Bournemouth, above.

Edith, too, had aged. Arthritis troubled her, and the couple moved every few years in search of a home that required less upkeep. The peaceful seaside town of Bournemouth held a special charm. Although Tolkien hated to leave the Oxford community, he knew Edith preferred Bournemouth. The move was made in 1968.

Although Tolkien had been kept busy with the publication of *The Lord of the Rings* and the family's frequent moves, he continued to work on *The Silmarillion.* He knew that Allen & Unwin truly wanted to publish it now. After all, *The Lord of the Rings* trilogy had sold millions of copies. In the United States, the books attracted a special following among college students. The volumes appeared on recommended reading lists and were discussed in literature classes.

An aerial view of Bournemouth, above, *and the main square and Grand Central Gardens,* below

Tolkien photographed during a moment of conversation

One professor in the United States wrote that his students rated Tolkien among England's three greatest authors, along with Shakespeare and Charles Dickens.

Every now and then, another Tolkien title appeared. None matched the popularity of the hobbit books, but each was an excellent piece of writing. Still, *The Silmarillion* waited to be finished.

In 1971, Tolkien resolved to complete the book, which he had begun in 1917. At his empty desk, he sat puffing on his pipe and studying notebooks and boxes full of papers. He pored carefully over all his notes and the chapters that he had written and rewritten so often.

Then something happened to delay his work. In the middle of November, Edith became ill. She was admitted to

At Merton College, Oxford

the hospital with an inflamed gallbladder, and on Monday, November 29, 1971, she died at the age of 82. Tolkien had lost his loving companion after 55 years of marriage.

There was no question of staying on in Bournemouth. That move had been made for Edith. By March 1972, Tolkien had taken up residence at 21 Merton Street in Oxford. His son John was a priest with his own parish, while Michael and Christopher had followed their father's footsteps into the classroom as teachers. Priscilla was working as a probation officer. All the children came often to visit their father.

Nor did the outside world choose to ignore the famed author. In the spring of 1972, Tolkien visited Buckingham Palace for an audience with Queen Elizabeth II. She presented him with a C.B.E. (Commander of the Order of the

*After Edith died, Tolkien returned to Oxford to live at 21 Merton St.
and often dined around the corner at the Eastgate Hotel.*

Tolkien with his walking stick, on the stairway of the Merton Street residence

Tolkien's study on Merton Street

British Empire) for his distinguished contributions to the literary arts. On June 4, he returned to Oxford to receive an Honorary Doctorate of Letters for his work in philology. The following June, he was off to Edinburgh, Scotland, for another honorary degree. And there were many more invitations, which he respectfully declined.

As the weeks passed, Tolkien's steps became slower, and he seemed to tire more quickly. Although he used to dash quickly through the crossword puzzles in the newspaper, now he cast them aside after completing only a few words. In late August 1973, Tolkien traveled to Bournemouth to visit friends. He complained of stomach cramps and was admitted to a private hospital. Doctors diagnosed an acute bleeding gastric ulcer, and the family was summoned. Michael and Christopher were out of the country, but John and Priscilla hurried to be with their father. After a brief recovery, Tolkien developed a chest infection. He died on Sunday morning, September 2, 1973, at the age of 81.

News of Tolkien's death saddened people around the world. "The earth is an emptier place without him," wrote one newspaper editor. "And Middle-earth is filled with sad-faced elves and hobbits."

Four days later, Father John Tolkien presided at the funeral mass for his father in Oxford. Family and friends gathered to pray for the man who had enriched their lives.

Four years later, in 1977, Christopher Tolkien guided to publication the volume his father had begun 60 years earlier. *The Silmarillion* quickly found its place among the other works created by the man who had earned the title "Master of Fantasy."

epiLogue

According to a list published in *U.S. News and World Report* in march 1990, *The Hobbit* and two volumes of *The Lord of the Rings* are among the 20 all-time best-selling paperbacks. J. R. R. Tolkien is the only author to have more than one book on the list. Tolkien's paperback publisher in the United States, Ballantine Books, reports that there are over 50 million copies of his works in print. Additional copies have been published in 40 other countries.

But numbers are only one indication of Tolkien's popularity. Recently, the word *hobbit* was entered in the *Oxford English Dictionary*. When Tolkien was working on the *New English Dictionary* so long ago, he probably never thought that he would make his own contribution to such a collection of words.

The gravestone of Edith and J.R.R. Tolkien recalls the story of Beren and Luthien Tinuviel, their favorite story because it was inspired by Ronald's love for Edith.

In the mid-1990s, New Line Cinema announced plans for the creation of film versions of the Lord of the Rings trilogy. In 2001, after much anticipation, the first of the three movies, *The Fellowship of the Ring,* was released. The film was an instant sensation and won four out of the thirteen Academy Awards for which it was nominated. The release of the film inspired a whole new wave of Tolkien-mania. Tolkien websites, Lord of the Rings action figures, and increased sales of Tolkien books worldwide are just a few examples of Tolkien's renewed and undying popularity. With the new century beginning, the literary legacy of J. R. R. Tolkien remains secure every place on earth—and in Middle-earth as well. Indeed, as so many graffiti artists have proclaimed, "Frodo lives."

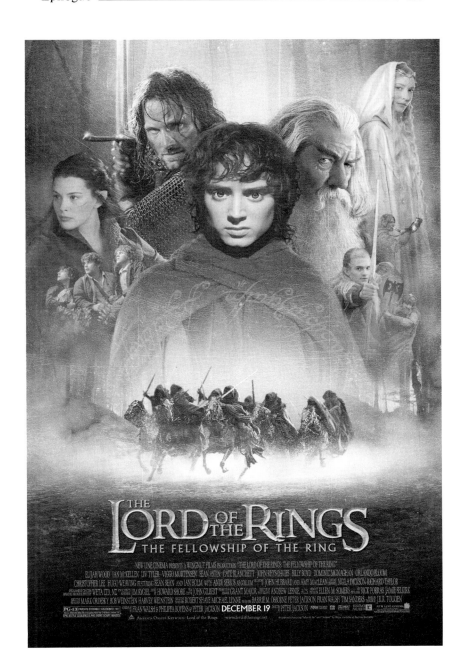

Milestones in the Life of J. J. R. Tolkien

1892   Born January 3 in Bloemfontein, South Africa

1894   Brother Hilary Arthur Reuel Tolkien born February 17

1895   Mabel Tolkien (mother) takes Ronald and Hilary to visit relatives in England.

1896   Arthur Tolkien (father) dies.

1900   Ronald enters King Edward's School.

1904   Mabel Tolkien dies.

1908   Ronald meets Edith Bratt.

1911   Ronald enters Exeter College, Oxford University.

1916   Ronald and Edith are married. Ronald is stationed in France but returns to England in November because of illness.

1917   Begins "The Book of Lost Tales," later called *The Silmarillion*. Birth of son John

1918   World War I ends. Ronald is discharged from service.

1920   Birth of son Michael. Accepts teaching position at Leeds University

1924   Birth of son Christopher

1925   Elected professor of Anglo-Saxon at Oxford

1929   Birth of daughter Priscilla

1930   Begins to write *The Hobbit*

1937   *The Hobbit* is published. Tolkien begins *The Lord of the Rings*.

1949   Completes *The Lord of the Rings. Farmer Giles* is published.

1954	Volumes 1 and 2 of *The Lord of the Rings* are published.
1955	Volume 3 is published.
1959	Tolkien retires from his professorship at Oxford.
1971	Edith Tolkien dies.
1972	Awarded the C.B.E.
1973	Tolkien dies on September 2 in Bournemouth, England.

Names and Terms from Middle-earth

Bilbo Baggins: a meek and mild, middle-aged hobbit who leads a group of dwarves to Lonely Mountain in an effort to reclaim their stolen treasure. He is the central character in *The Hobbit*, published in 1937.

dwarves: stocky, humanlike creatures who mine gold and silver and pride themselves on their jewel-laden homes. For the most part, they stick to themselves unless their code of justice is violated.

elves: elves are the oldest creatures in Middle-earth, where they have great power through their senses of sight and sound. Sensitive and strong, elves show a deep love for nature, especially for trees.

ents: guardians of trees in the Middle-earth realm. Combining the physical features of men and trees, ents are capable of great physical power and strength when moved to action, but generally they are sluggish.

The Fellowship of the Ring: the first book in *The Lord of the Rings* trilogy

Frodo Baggins: a cousin of Bilbo Baggins who becomes the central hobbit character in *The Lord of the Rings* trilogy. Frodo proves himself both brave and resourceful.

hobbits: furry-footed little people who inhabit Tolkien's realm of Middle-earth. "I am in fact a hobbit," the author wrote, "in all but size." He meant that hobbits were rather ordinary and plain, but capable of great imagination and of reaching beyond themselves for adventure.

The Lord of the Rings: Tolkien's three-volume fantasy, which includes *The Fellowship of the Ring*, *The Two Towers*, and *The Return of the King*

men: less important characters during the early Middle-earth period. They seem destined to become more powerful than elves and dwarves.

Middle-earth: the setting for Tolkien's fantasies and myths. Although some readers think of Middle-earth as another planet, the author emphatically affirms that "Middle-earth is *our* world" in another time when human life was different.

orcs: creatures, evil in thought and behavior, better known as goblins

The Return of the King: the third book in *The Lord of the Rings* trilogy. (Tolkien disliked this title because he felt it gave the story line away.)

The Silmarillion: a collection of myths and legends. Begun in 1917 as "The Book of Lost Tales," this was Tolkien's effort to provide England with its own mythology. *The Silmarillion* was not published until 1977, four years after Tolkien's death.

Bibliography

Bingham, Jane M., ed. *Writers for Children*. New York: Charles Scribner's Sons, 1988.

Carpenter, Humphrey. *J. R. R. Tolkien: A Biography*. London: Allen & Unwin, 1977; Boston: Houghton Mifflin Co., 1977.

Commire, Anne, ed. *Something about the Author*. Vol. 32. Detroit: Gale Research, 1983.

Giddings, Robert, ed. *J. R. R. Tolkien: This Far Land*. New York: Barnes and Noble, 1984.

Helms, Randel. *Tolkien's World*. Boston: Houghton Mifflin Co., 1975.

Kocher, Paul. *Master of Middle-earth: The Achievement of J. R. R. Tolkien*. Boston: Houghton Mifflin Co., 1972.

Rogers, Deborah Webster and A. Ivor. *J. R .R. Tolkien*. Boston: Twayne Publishers, 1980.

Tyler, J. E. A., ed. *The New Tolkien Companion*. New York: St. Martin's Press, 1979.

For Further Reading

Tolkien, John Ronald Reuel. *The Hobbit, or There and Back Again*. London: Allen & Unwin, 1937; Boston: Houghton Mifflin Co., 1938.

_____. *Farmer Giles of Ham*. London: Allen & Unwin, 1949; Boston: Houghton Mifflin Co., 1950.

_____. *The Fellowship of the Ring*. Vol. 1, *The Lord of the Rings*. London: Allen & Unwin, 1954; Boston: Houghton Mifflin Co., 1955.

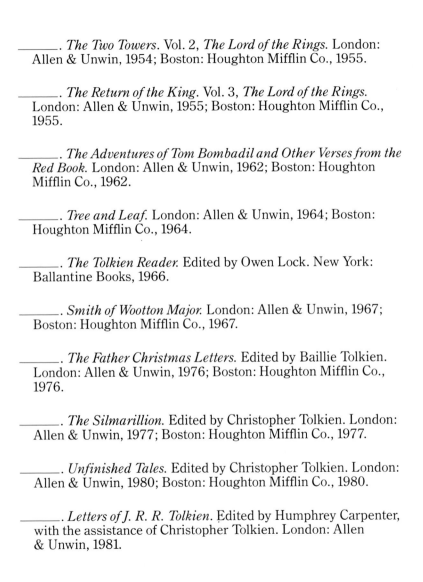

_____. *The Two Towers.* Vol. 2, *The Lord of the Rings.* London: Allen & Unwin, 1954; Boston: Houghton Mifflin Co., 1955.

_____. *The Return of the King.* Vol. 3, *The Lord of the Rings.* London: Allen & Unwin, 1955; Boston: Houghton Mifflin Co., 1955.

_____. *The Adventures of Tom Bombadil and Other Verses from the Red Book.* London: Allen & Unwin, 1962; Boston: Houghton Mifflin Co., 1962.

_____. *Tree and Leaf.* London: Allen & Unwin, 1964; Boston: Houghton Mifflin Co., 1964.

_____. *The Tolkien Reader.* Edited by Owen Lock. New York: Ballantine Books, 1966.

_____. *Smith of Wootton Major.* London: Allen & Unwin, 1967; Boston: Houghton Mifflin Co., 1967.

_____. *The Father Christmas Letters.* Edited by Baillie Tolkien. London: Allen & Unwin, 1976; Boston: Houghton Mifflin Co., 1976.

_____. *The Silmarillion.* Edited by Christopher Tolkien. London: Allen & Unwin, 1977; Boston: Houghton Mifflin Co., 1977.

_____. *Unfinished Tales.* Edited by Christopher Tolkien. London: Allen & Unwin, 1980; Boston: Houghton Mifflin Co., 1980.

_____. *Letters of J. R. R. Tolkien.* Edited by Humphrey Carpenter, with the assistance of Christopher Tolkien. London: Allen & Unwin, 1981.

INDEX

Merton College, 88
Morgan, Father Francis, 24, 27-28, 32-33, 38-40, 50
Morgoth, 67

New English Dictionary, The, 68, 71-72

Old and Middle English, 23, 31, 32
Old Norse, 32, 66
orcs, 66
Oxford University, 38-40, 45, 50, 74-75, 83-84, 91, 92, 99
Oxford Honor School of English Language and Literature, 50

Reynolds, R.W., 45
Roos, 67

St. Phillip's Catholic School, 20
Sarehole, 18, 19
Shakespeare, William, 37, 94
Sheridan, Richard Brinsley, 47
Sir Gawain and the Green Knight, 31-32, 42, 73
Silmarillion, The, see Tolkien, writing
Smith, G.B., 59, 61, 66
Smaug, 78
Suffield, Beatrice, 27
Suffield, Grandfather, 13, 17
Suffield, Mabel, see Mabel Tolkien

T.C.B.S., (Tea Club Barrow's Stores) 42, 47, 59, 61, 63

Tolkien, Arthur, 10-15, 17
Tolkien, Christopher, 74-75, 83, 85, 90, 95, 99
Tolkien, Edith (Bratt), 35-36, 38-39, 49, 53, 56-58, 61, 65-68, 72, 74, 76, 88, 92, 94-95
Tolkien, Hilary, 12-13, 17, 24, 27, 32, 39
Tolkien, John, 67-68, 75, 77, 95, 99
Tolkien, J.R.R.,
  birth, 10
  early childhood, 10, 12, 13, 17-20
  early interests, 18
  enters King Edward's School, 19
  education, 19-25, 28-32, 36-43
  invents languages, 31, 65, 67
  at Lyme Regis, 32-33
  meets Edith Bratt, 35
  as a debater, 36-37, 41
  fails entrance test for Oxford, 39
  at Oxford University, 45-57
    wins scholarship, 40
    arrives at, 45
    elected president of debating society, 53
    wins Skeat prize for English, 53
    graduates from, 57
  engagement to Edith, 53
  trip to Cornwall, 53
  marriage to Edith, 58
  military service, 57-68
  begins stories, 66
  end of war, 68
  as lexicographer, 68, 71-72
  as tutor, 72